FROM
THE
HEART

A 40 Day Journey
of Experiencing God's Love
in Everyday Life

Sharon Guillory

KS Media and Publishing Company

PO Box 459

Cypress, Texas 77410, USA

Contents

Acknowledgements

To my parents, Hilbert Sr. and Mary Guillory: Thank you for your love and support. Your faithfulness set me on a journey to know God for who He is. You taught me how to love. I love you both most dearly.

To my brothers, Hilbert Jr. and Hilton: It is the strength of who you are that have strengthened me through my years. We have a bond that grows with each passing day. I love you tremendously.

To my brother, Kevin: I miss you more than words can say. I love you, Bro!

To my twin sister, Karon: Words cannot express the love I have for you. I consider you to be my very best friend and my other half.

To my nieces and nephews, Aaron, Ashley, Briana, Kevin, and Aubree: You bring so much joy into my life. I love you so much!

To my sister-in-law, Julie: Thank you for being my sister and such a special part of our family. I love you.

To my uncle, James August: Thank you for your prayers and being a spiritual mentor. Your encouragement and support mean the world to me.

To Pastor Kirbyjon Caldwell: Your teaching through the years has been an integral part of my spiritual growth. I sincerely thank you for being my Pastor.

To my editor, Adrienne E Bell: Your encouragement, your knowledge, and your friendship have made this book a reality. Thank you for being such a blessing in my life. I wish God's most wonderful blessings for you and your family.

Sharon Guillory

To all of my relatives, friends, and associates: Thank you for the support and encouragement. I wish God's many blessings for you all.

Most importantly, I want to thank my Lord and Savior, Jesus Christ: This project has been a "labor of love". You are the keeper of my soul and the very air that I breathe. My love for you is the core of who I am. Thank you, God, for this journey. It is my sincere honor to share your love with the world.

Dedication

This book is dedicated to my wonderful and supportive family, without whom this book would not have been possible. Mom and Dad, I thank you for showing me who God is by just being who you are. To my brothers, twin sister, and sister-in law, thank you for being the best friends I could ever have. To my nieces and nephews, you fill my heart with joy.

From deep within my heart – I love you all.

FOREWORD

Greetings! You are about to embark on an exciting life-changing trip and all you have to bring with you is your commitment to be present, open and willing to act on what you read. From beginning to end, you will find Sharon to be a gifted author, teacher and tour guide.

In the pages ahead, you will benefit from Sharon's lifelong allegiance to loving God and serving others. She offers you a wealth of simple, practical guidance that will enable you to experience God more abundantly each day you live. As you travel through the *40-Day Journey of Experiencing God's Love in Everyday Life*, you will be encouraged to assess your life and how well you use it to share God's love with others. With Sharon's help as a friend and confidant, you will also work through the "small" things you encounter that can affect you in a big way.

The Lord loves you just as you are...and He will bless you mightily as you put greater focus on Him and His will for the next 40 days and beyond. Bon voyage!

Pastor Kirbyjon Caldwell

The Windsor Village Church Family

Houston, Texas

Introduction

The goal of this 40 Day Journey is to take the simplest scenarios and relate them from a Christian perspective. At the end of this amazing journey, you will see God in EVERYTHING: Nature, Technology, Business, Education and even LAUGHTER. You will see God's heart toward you revealed in more ways than you could ever imagine...40 ways to be exact! We often envision God sitting on a gigantic throne looking down at us but not really interested in the details of our lives. Have you ever said, "God, what should I wear to work?" or "What route should I take to my destination?" This daily walk highlighting God's good heart towards us will constantly remind you, what concerns us, concerns Him. When we are going through our struggles and trials, we may not see Him like we think we should but in many cases we aren't looking for Him. In most cases, we aren't taking the time to see or feel Him. But when you fail some of life's tests, sometimes that's God. Even getting caught in the rain, God may get the credit for that too. At the end of every single day, we must realize this life is not about us. If we would only take the time to look and feel Him at every turn, if we would only take the time to see Him operate through every trial and every test in life, we would realize He was there all the time.

Let's take this beautiful journey together and experience God's love in everyday life, from my heart to yours.

Situations, sounds and circumstances
have a way of competing for our attention.
God should never have to compete for my time or yours.

DAY ONE

QUIET TIME

I once read a book called, "*Celebration of Discipline*" by Richard J. Foster. The book was about several key practices or disciplines of the Christian faith. Two of the principles addressed were solitude and meditation, or "quiet time".

Before I read the book, I thought of quiet time as time alone or of being by myself. I paid no attention to the television that's always on until I fall asleep or the radio playing in my car every time I start the engine. Even in my office, I had to have the radio on while I worked. The only quiet in my life was during sleep.

One Saturday morning at home I decided to turn off the TV and the radio for a little while. First, I listened. I heard nothing. The quiet was surprisingly unfamiliar. What to do and where to go were questions that I asked myself. After a few moments I heard a sound that I had not heard in a long, long time. It was the sound of birds singing. I could not remember the last time I heard the sound of singing birds outside my window. I then realized that the birds had been chirping for quite some time but they could not be heard due to all the "noise" around me. Until I removed all the sounds and distractions, I could not hear what was going on just a few feet outside my door.

Those quiet moments helped me put things in perspective. I realized that the simplicity and serenity that I felt was so available to me and I didn't even know it. The flip of a few switches from "on" to "off" allowed me the chance to hear and to feel, a chance to clear my head. I didn't hear all the noise until the noise was actually gone. Once I cleared the clamor then I received the calm.

Situations, sounds and circumstances have a way of competing for our attention. God should never have to compete for my time or yours. So many times God can answer our questions and/or our prayers but we just can't hear Him because of all the "stuff" around us. It's not a matter of hours of silence; it is just a few mellow moments spent in reflection. It's removing the ruckus to renew your mind.

One Saturday morning I heard God playing music outside my window. It was the sweet song of singing birds that a few silent moments allowed my heart to hear. God should never have to shout to reach us, only His whisper should do. It's a whisper that can only be heard during moments of silence, only during quiet time…

We have all heard countless times that everything happens for a reason. But we all must learn to trust God when things DON'T happen.

DAY TWO

NO

Most of us assume the word, "*no*" to have a negative connotation. In most instances, we are correct in that assumption. At other times "no" could leave us feeling despondent or rejected from not getting what we want or maybe getting what we don't want.

Have you ever earnestly prayed to God for something but His answer is emphatically but lovingly "NO"? Have you ever then asked God for the same thing but in a different way thinking you could change His mind?

What about the job that you applied for, had a great interview and were sure that the job was yours only to find out that the position was offered to another applicant? Or maybe you placed a bid on a house you wanted to purchase only to discover that another bid was accepted.

There have been many times when I have questioned God's refusal to answer a prayer. Then I try to analyze or rationalize His denial. I try to figure out God's reasoning as if I could actually "decode" His declination. For example, I remember a time when I was intent on visiting my parents one holiday weekend. My plan was to leave on Saturday morning and return early Monday morning. Every weather report for that particular time span predicted heavy rain. The drive was only 150 miles and I figured that since I had made the trip so many times that the weather was not really an issue so in spite of the predicted bad weather, I made my first attempt on Saturday morning. There was no rain when I started on my journey but as soon as I got on the highway I had to turn around and come back home due to heavy thunderstorms.

The strangest thing was not the fact that I had to cancel my trip due to stormy weather but that the rain had *completely stopped* as soon as I parked my car in my garage. In the back of my mind I questioned why God would stop me dead in my tracks when my only intent was to visit my Dad for Father's Day. The next day, Sunday, I again decided to make the trip to visit my parents and return home on Monday morning. No matter how hard I tried for some reason I could not seem to hit the road.

After toiling the entire weekend about my inability to make the trip to visit my parents, I finally had to concede. Finally, after two days, I decided to just trust God. You would think that I would know by now that God had a specific reason for disrupting my plans. It was not until the very next day, Monday, that all was revealed. I was awakened early that morning by strong winds and heavy rain. Then I heard loud thunder and saw reflections of lightning through my windows. Immediately I turned on the news and saw actual footage of massive flooding on the *very interstate highway* on which I _would have been_ traveling on my return trip from visiting my parents (remember – my plan was to return on Monday morning).

God, in His foresight and infinite wisdom, knew that had I followed through with MY plans instead of His, I would have literally been stuck in a flood on the very highway that I was watching on the morning news. When God said "NO" to my travel plans, He was actually protecting me. Upon that realization, the only thing I could do was to turn off the television, get on my knees, and thank God for an *unanswered* prayer.

We have all heard countless times that everything happens for a reason. But we all must learn to trust God when things DON'T happen. A friend once told me that what we think of as rejection may very well be God's loving protection. Thinking back, there have been numerous other occasions where God's refusal actually meant tremendous blessings. I'm learning that when God says "*no*" to my will, it is up to me to say "*yes*" to His. It is not only a matter of trusting that God knows what is best for us but it is also learning to thank God that He loves us enough to just say, *"NO"*…

Celebrate the little victories along your road to success. Before you place too much emphasis on "the big picture", make a mental marker of all the milestones you have overcome.

DAY THREE

DON'T LOOK AT THE BIG PICTURE

One day, I decided to walk four miles on my treadmill. Just the *thought* of four miles seemed too long and too difficult. So instead of focusing on the entire distance, I decided to focus on one mile at a time.

So often we have a tendency to focus on the big picture. In doing so we tend to forget about all the "milestone moments" in between. It is the little triumphs along our journey that we frequently lose sight of, triumphs that go unnoticed and unrecognized.

Have you ever known a runner in a race that constantly stares at the finish line? Instead a runner must focus on the task at hand – running as fast as he can and finishing the race. Each lap or mile completed brings him one step closer to the winner's circle. For a marathoner, each mile marker passed are miniature milestones, they are accomplishments that can accelerate achievement.

As I finished my walk, I realized that I would never have started my walk had I only focused on the big picture, the entire distance to be walked. The only way my goal could have been achieved was by taking one mile at a time. Each completed mile encouraged me to keep going until my goal was reached. Instead of looking at the big picture, in my mind I focused on the minuscule milestones of each mile as I made my way toward completion.

Whatever your dreams, your goals, your aspirations for the future, take time to meditate on your monumental moments. Celebrate the little victories along your road to success. Before you place too much emphasis on "the big picture", make a mental marker of all the milestones you have overcome. In doing so, the big picture may not seem too big to reach but only a snapshot of your triumphs to come.

God may just be waiting for us to remove the roadblocks that are keeping us from receiving His best.

DAY FOUR

Blocking Your Own Blessings

We, as children of God, are blessed by the very nature of who we are in Christ. It is God's will to shower blessings on each one of us. But there are times in our life when we block our blessings by our words and actions. An unforgiving heart, a bitter spirit, or an angry countenance can hinder our blessings.

When the Israelites were freed from slavery in Egypt, God promised His people a land flowing with milk and honey. Gratitude and thanksgiving were in the hearts of a whole **nation** of people. They were on a journey to the Promised Land. Somewhere along the way, when the road got too rough, too long, and too burdensome, the Israelites grew weary. They soon became enamored in iniquity and rebellion. It took the Israelites 40 years to receive a blessing from God that maybe could have taken only 40 days. Rebellion caused them to block their own blessings.

God blesses us to be a blessing to other people. But sin in our own life can indeed hinder the blessings that could have been bestowed on someone else. It is one thing to hinder our own blessings but to forfeit God's favor being bestowed on others is much more tragic. It's like a stalled car on a busy freeway. The road ahead seems free and clear. All of a sudden the flow of traffic comes to a dead stop. You cannot see that far ahead so you have to sit there and wonder what's going on. After creeping along for several miles you finally see what the problem is. It is one stalled car blocking and halting traffic for miles back. That one stalled car is the same as rebellion that can stop the flow of blessings for many others that may follow behind us.

You never know how many blessings are just around the corner. But God may just be waiting for us to remove the roadblocks that are keeping us from receiving His best. Remove the blockades to blessings and receive what God has for you today. What are you waiting for?

Sometimes we can choose to be happy or we can choose to focus on our problems without even realizing it.

DAY FIVE

CHOICES

Someone once told me that we all are where we are at this very moment because of the choices and decisions we've made in our lives. The job you have, the church you attend, or even the food you eat are based on choices and decisions that we make daily. Sometimes even your frame of mind can be a choice. Sometimes we can choose to be happy or we can choose to focus on our problems without even realizing it.

I remember going to the doctor once for a physical examination and discovered that my cholesterol was high. Honestly, I was not surprised. At that point it dawned on me that my cholesterol was high mainly because of my eating *choices*. Two weeks prior to my physical I had already decided to eliminate fried foods from my diet. That was a *choice*. I realized that I had to make *lifelong choices* that affect my health.

What about our spiritual choices? Whether we know it or not, we make spiritual choices constantly. Remember that inner voice that told you to do this or that? Did you listen to that inner voice or did you *choose* to ignore it? First we must decipher who is speaking to us in our spirit before that choice can be made. Is it God or is it the enemy? I have done both - I have made choices to listen to my spirit and not to listen. Some choices were good and some were not so good.

Even our *simplest choices* can make or break someone's day. You never know where people are in their lives on a daily basis. YOUR smile could brighten someone's day. YOUR kind word could encourage someone this day. YOUR hug could comfort someone today. These are all *mindless choices* that we make that could brighten the day of someone else.

God gives us all the freedom of choice. It is our choices that determine where we are in our lives and the nature of our relationship with God. But wisdom comes from seeking God prior to making decisions. And that choice is totally up to you. What choice will you make?

There are times when we turn off our own internal GPS thinking that we know where we're going and how to get there. It is not until we make a wrong turn or get redirected that we realize that we are lost and need direction.

DAY SIX

G-P-S (GOD'S POSITIONING SYSTEM)

I must say that my sense of direction is greatly lacking. I cannot tell you in what direction I'm driving, or if I'm facing north, south, east, or west as I stand. Driving to an unfamiliar location in a big city can definitely be a challenge. So to make my life a little easier, I bought a global positioning system (GPS) for my car.

I was so excited when my niece set it up for me (really, all she had to do was plug it in). Everywhere I went, I used my GPS to get me to my final destination. It shows the direction in which I drive, my speed, and even an estimated time of arrival. To top it all off, it even verbally tells you when to turn, where to turn, and will "re-calculate" if you go off course.

As believers in Christ, we have our own GPS (<u>God's</u> positioning system), called Holy Spirit. Our own internal GPS will tell us where to go and will even warn us when we we're going in the wrong direction.

Let me be really truthful about the GPS I have in my car: There are many times I don't want to hear what it has to say. I don't want to turn when it tells me to because I have my own route in my head of exactly how to get to where I'm going. But that's what you and I do with God. God has a path already chosen for each one of us and all we have to do is follow His directions. When we don't want to listen, we just tune Him out and go our own way. But thinking I know what's best and I know how to get to where I'm going, I completely go in the opposite direction of where God is leading me. So many times I find myself taking a journey that God never intended for me to take.

Let me give you an example of taking *my own* journey. It was

September 2005 and it was forecasted that a hurricane was approaching the Houston area. I decided that the best thing to do was to head east to my parents' home in Louisiana. It is usually just a two and a half hour trip so I made no provisions for food and only took two bottles of water since I thought it would be a very short trip. It was really early in the morning so I figured that I would reach my destination before lunch, before I got hungry. I also decided to take a thoroughfare rather than the major highway to avoid heavy traffic.

So here I am, driving along the highway, traffic is not bad, and I think I'm running from Hurricane Rita. Did it dawn on me to tune my radio to the news? No. I wanted to listen to music because I already knew what I was doing – I was escaping the danger of a hurricane, on my way to the safety of my parents' home. I had it all figured out – or so I thought.

The trip was going very smoothly until traffic came to a complete stop. I sat in one spot for what seemed like an eternity. I literally traveled a half mile in two hours. Suddenly I approached a road block and was re-directed to unfamiliar territory. I panicked because there I was – traveling alone, no food, little water, and was re-directed by the State Police to travel in a completely different direction. I was lost and had no GPS to tell me how to get to my parents' house or to my own house. The ONLY thing I could do was to say a prayer and ask for direction which is what I should have done before I started on my "journey".

Needless to say, my prayer was answered and soon I found my way and decided to just go back home. A trip that normally would have taken me two and a half hours, actually took me NINE hours to complete. But that's not the most important part of the story. Remember I said that I decided to listen to music rather than the news because I *"knew what I was doing"*? It was not until I returned home tired, hungry, thirsty, and with little gas in my car, that I discovered that *while* I was "escaping the hurricane", it had changed its course and was headed *DIRECTLY* to the place I was trying so hard to get to. Hurricane Rita hit Louisiana the very next day! Suddenly, it was my parents' safety that I so desperately prayed for rather than my own.

Would it have made a difference if I had a global positioning system in my car as I headed toward danger? No, it would have made no difference because a GPS cannot tell you if weather danger lies ahead; it only tells you how to get from point A to point B. It was *God's* positioning system that spared me. He knew that I was not running from a threat, but TO a threat. When I made the decision to go back home I had no idea I was headed toward the storm. I decided to return home because I was tired of driving and because my trip was re-directed. God had "re-calculated" my journey to get me back to safety.

There are times when we turn off our own internal GPS thinking that we know where we're going and how to get there. It is not until we make a wrong turn or get redirected that we realize that we are lost and need direction. But sometimes it's not the destination but the journey that is most important. It is not our own sense of direction that will get us to our destination but rather God's positioning that will lead us in the way that we should go. It is when we move towards God that we find shelter from the storms of life. As we listen to His voice and follow His lead it is then that God positions us to receive His absolute best.

*What at times may feel like rejection is
in reality God's loving protection.*

DAY SEVEN

DO NOT OPEN

Have you ever tried to open a locked door without the key? Have you ever prayed for something but you just could not seem to get a clear answer to your prayer?

There was a time when I had been attempting to do just that – I was trying to open a door that God wanted to remain closed. I had been praying for guidance on one specific request. No matter how hard I prayed, it felt as if I could not get clarity from God.

After praying, fasting, and much frustration I sought counsel from a very dear friend, a prayer partner. Thankfully she would not advise me until she also prayed about my "dilemma". The answer that I received from her is the answer that I had received from God from the very beginning.

So many times our responses from God do not coincide with our own wants and wishes. My friend received the same answer from God that I had received all along. The answer we both heard from God had nothing to do with what I wanted or felt I needed. God's reply had *everything* to do with the matter of my focus and *nothing* to do with the situation about which I had prayed. I was so busy making His answer fit into a little box that I truly lost focus on Him. I had given God three choices: should I do this, should I do that, or should I do nothing at all. You would think that I have learned by now that God is much too big for my "little boxes."

I finally realized that God had already given me the key to the locked door that I kept running up against, trying to open it on my own. From day one, God had been holding out His hand with the key to my "locked door" but I just refused to take hold.

The key to my quandary was to *just <u>trust</u> God.* Trusting God will open every locked door, every sealed window and every impenetrable heart. Trusting Him was all that was required. I had to first trust God that <u>*He*</u> knows what is best for me. His plans for me could very well have been postponed or delayed had He granted the desire of my heart.

Next, I had to let God be God without boxing Him in. I imagined in my mind God lovingly shaking His head at how incredibly finite my deliberations had been. I can see Him being pleasantly amused at the restrictions I had put on Him, the Creator of the universe.

If you are wondering if God has unlocked that door, the answer is no. But I am learning to thank Him for His refusal. Why? Because if the door had been opened, there is a great possibility that what I thought to be best for me could have very well meant many missed opportunities.

What at times may feel like rejection is in reality God's loving protection. When God refuses to unlock one door, it may be so that He can open the many windows of Heaven to bestow on you more blessings than you could ever imagine. The *key* is to just *trust* God...

Communing with God is our shield from the showers.

DAY EIGHT

DOWN CAME THE RAIN

We have all experienced times of drought – when land gets parched due to a lack of rain, the sun blazes, a dry wind blows, and the heat seems unbearable. We may also go through times of *spiritual* drought - when it seems as if we do not pray as much or our prayers themselves seem dry and parched.

Drought is defined as a period of dry weather or an extended shortage. *Spiritual* drought can therefore mean a time when our prayers are "dry" and emotionless, or an extended period of time when we do not pray at all. The only way to reverse a drought is through rain, usually in abundance. Parched land needs a large amount of rain that not only reaches the ground but enough precipitation that goes far below the surface. Just as the earth must become fully saturated before the effects of a drought can be reversed, it is our hearts that must become fully saturated with prayer, praise, and the love of God for the termination of a spiritual drought.

But what causes a spiritual drought? What type of "rain" saturates the heart? A spiritual deficiency can oftentimes be a result of complacency, when everything is going good and all seems right in the world. We tend to forget about prayer when we are happy and content. We work, we play, we travel, we go to school, and we become busy just living the best way we know how. Our lack of prayer can actually go unrecognized — until suddenly *down comes the rain.*

We all know that God is not the author of confusion. We also know that God takes delight in blessing His children. But there are times when we must be reminded that we have a God in heaven who wants a relationship with us no matter how good or how bad things are going in our lives. God knows that when the "rain" comes, we will then come to Him.

One day, I went running on a sunny afternoon. The weather was beautiful – not too hot and not too cool. I had just reached the halfway point of my run when it started to slightly drizzle. As I immediately turned around and headed home the rain suddenly began to come down in droves. The rain was now pouring down and I still had a mile and a half before I made it back home. There was no shelter from the rain so the only thing I could do was try to hurry back. Running made the rain go into my eyes and I could not see; merely walking made my time in the rain much longer. I decided to run for a while then walk for a while until my journey was over.

When I got home I realized that I had never walked nor run in the rain for an extended length of time. I thought about what it felt like not to have any shelter from the storm. I was completely exposed to nature's elements with no refuge, no safe haven – *down came the rain* and down came my defenses. A lack of prayer can leave us vulnerable and unprotected just like getting caught in the rain with no umbrella. Communing with God is our shield from the showers.

None of us are immune to times of spiritual drought. But when God allows the storms of life to bring us back to Him, it is not to drench us with doubt or uncertainty. When we are in the midst of a downpour, our Father wants us to seek refuge in no one or nothing but Him. He alone is our shelter from the storms. Walking with God means that when *"down comes the rain"*, then *down comes God's protection*, our shelter from the storm.

Psalm 91: 4 states *"He will shield you with His wings. He will shelter you with His feathers. His faithful promises are your armor and protection."* So don't wait for the rain to come before you turn to God. He will wrap His loving arms around you rain or shine. God is waiting for you to come out of the rain...

Even in the midst of the most powerful weather system known to man, God still provides a peace inexplicable to human comprehension.

DAY NINE

EYE OF THE STORM

Hurricanes are called the greatest storms on earth. The name "hurricane" comes from "Huracan", the god of big winds and evil spirits once worshipped by the Mayan people of Central America. The word hurricane itself means "evil spirits."

One of the oddest things about hurricanes is the *eye of the storm.* In the very center of the storm system lies an area up to 25 miles across that is remarkably calm and serene. The eye of a hurricane consists of blue sky overhead surrounded by a wall of angry clouds. The strongest winds are in the eye wall.

I have always thought that God is the author of all weather phenomenon – hurricanes included. To merely consider the meaning of the word along with the nature of the storm, I now have a different outlook. God created a perfect world – no hurricanes, no tornadoes, no earthquakes. When man fell into sin, the very balance of nature became off kilter. The fall of man brought about the fall of nature.

Two hurricane survivors described the sounds of the winds as the storm passed directly overhead. Usually we hear accounts that the sounds are similar to that of a freight train. But what was most interesting to me was their description of the resonance of the hurricane winds. The sounds of a pack of angry dogs growling in fury and rage were most surprising. It was a sound that remains ever most in their memory. It was then that I knew that God was not the source of their experience. It was at that exact moment that I also realized that it was God and God alone that allowed them to survive those angry winds.

There is nothing evil about the God we serve. Sure God has a wrath, but even the wrath of God is wrought with love and kindness. Even in the midst of the most powerful weather system known to man, God still provides a peace inexplicable to human comprehension. It is called the *eye of the storm.* Ships at sea have been known to survive hurricanes by riding them out in the eye of a hurricane.

Sharon Guillory

In a turbulent world full of sorrow and despair, pain and disappointment, children of God can rest in God's eye, that is, the *eye of the storm*. He is our refuge, a safe haven in the very midst of the violent winds that surround the storms of life. In the very center of a hurricane, the eye, is where peace and tranquility lie. If we keep God as our center, then the eye wall (the strongest and most destructive winds) of life can cause us no harm. The calm center, the perfect peace that God provides is far more powerful than the most destructive and devastating forces of nature.

When dark clouds hang overhead and you hear the rumbling of an impending storm, you don't have to run *from* the storm. You just need to go to the *center* of it – the *eye of the storm*. Remaining God-centered is our only sanctuary. Letting God be the *eye* of *your* storm may very well be the difference between calm and calamity. It is God who is our source of perfect peace in the midst of angry winds during the storms of life. Keeping your eyes on God allows you to reside in the *eye of the storm...*

And he arose, and rebuked the wind, and said unto the sea, "Peace, be still." And the wind ceased, and there was a great calm. (Mark 4:39, King James Version)

Apart from God, we have no reflection at all.
Mankind was created in the very image of God, therefore,
our own reflection will always mirror His.

DAY TEN

THE FACE IN THE MIRROR

Seeing your reflection is something you may do thoughtlessly on a daily basis but what are you really looking at? What do those eyes say as you gaze in the mirror? Where does that smile come from as you ponder your mirrored image? I remember a time when my own reflection in the mirror was almost invisible due to low self-esteem and insecurity. Imagine staring at something but seeing nothing at all. My mirrored image was just that – a likeness in a mirror, void of confidence and self-assurance.

Finally, I just grew tired of trying to see past the fog that clouded my reflection. So one day as I was leaving work, a dear friend called me right before I walked out of my office. I told her that I could no longer live in the shadow of insecurity. It was time that I cleared the clouds of doubt and break the chains of fear that stagnated me for so very long. She immediately suggested that there was only one thing for me to do. My friend said that I should pray for God to show me what God sees when <u>He</u> looks at me.

I remember that it was a Wednesday afternoon around 5 pm. I had already put my purse on my shoulder and was ready to walk out my office door when my friend phoned me. After our conversation I closed my office door and said a brief prayer. I asked God one simple question, "God, what do <u>YOU</u> see when You see me." I then opened my office door, put my purse back on my shoulder, and went home. Needless to say, it did not take me long to forget my very short prayer. After two days, I still had no recollection of my prayer request. Then came the third day!

It was a beautiful Saturday morning and I was getting ready

to drive to a wedding out of town. I stopped at a nearby fast food restaurant, ate a quick breakfast, and was on my way. But first I needed to wash my hands, so into the restroom I went. As I dried my hands, I looked in the mirror while still in the lavatory. My face was glowing as I looked in the mirror. There was a white aura that surrounded my entire face. Instinctively, but for some unknown reason, I smiled. My teeth were pearly white as I looked in that mirror. Next, at that exact moment, God spoke to me and said, "Sharon, that's what I see when I see you. You are beautiful!" It was then that I remembered my prayer. Just three days earlier I had asked God to show me what He sees when He looks at me. It was then that the chains of doubt and insecurity were broken.

So many times, we think the world sees us the way we see ourselves. We even tend to carry ourselves according to our own perception of how and who we are. The most beautiful people in the world can feel the most unappealing and insecure and will carry themselves as such. One of the thinnest persons in a room that perceives himself or herself as large can begin to wear bigger clothes to hide what they perceive as a large frame. Their view is not reality; it is only a perception of their reflection.

But does God deal with perception or does He deal with reality? God sees us as who we really are. We are the very reflection of God Himself. We do not define who we are, but God defines ALL! The only reason that I hesitated in writing this devotional is because of the fear of perceived vanity. But the only purpose of this story is to relay the beauty of who <u>God</u> is. If we can see ourselves and others as God sees us, then the true beauty of who we are *in Him* will always shine forth. Apart from God, we have no reflection at all. Mankind was created in the very image of God, therefore our own reflection will always mirror His.

Prayerfully ask God to show you what <u>He</u> sees when He sees you and have faith in that prayer. Then when God does show you your beautiful reflection, you will always remember *the face in the mirror...*

...tests in life are endured to examine our faith because without tests, then there can be no testimonies.

DAY ELEVEN

TESTED

It was supposed to be a great Thanksgiving Holiday as I had just finished my final semester of graduate school. Two years and two months had seemed like an eternity as I was determined to finish the program with a perfect GPA. I had taken my last exam in the entire program the night before I was to drive home to visit my parents for the Holiday. The exam was administered electronically so my test score popped up as soon as I clicked "Submit".

You cannot imagine the relief I felt that this final test was an open-book exam as my brain was exhausted from over two years of writing papers and reports, creating and giving presentations, and turning in homework while maintaining a full-time job. This last class was an online course that seemed to be one of the most difficult even though the class was allowed to work in study groups of four students each. For six weeks our study group turned in assignments with absolutely no feedback from our professor. With charts, graphs, countless paragraphs, and weekly deadlines looming overhead, homework was being submitted with mere silence in return. On the very day of my final exam, I had NO idea of my grades in this course.

So here I am, sitting at my computer, mentally exhausted but also ecstatic to complete the last phase of a very long journey. Going into the exam, I felt prepared and confident. Over two hours of flipping pages, perusing data, and answering countless multiple choice questions were tedious tasks that certainly were not to be envied.

Did I review the answers that I was about to submit? Yes. Did I feel confident about my answers? Yes. Was I ready to get this process completed? YES!!!! I finally clicked on the "Submit" button and my final test score appeared without hesitation – much to my dismay. My FINAL TEST SCORE WAS "*66*". My heart sank lower than the bottom of my feet. I was devastated as any shot of a perfect GPA was gone for good. Two years striving for my own personal goal had vanished with the simple click of a computer mouse. However, there was one fact that I could not forget that God kept bringing to the forefront – I took this test alone and whatever grade I received was my very own!

Even though this particular class was specifically designed for students to work in groups of four, my study group instead decided to take the test independently rather than as a group simply to maintain integrity. We knew that in a regular classroom setting, group test-taking was strictly prohibited. And even though this course was conducted online, maintaining honesty was of the utmost importance. Thus, any grade we received was to be an individual grade, not a collective one.

Finally, I had to accept the fact that the academic goal that I had set for myself was history! Not only did I not pass the exam, but I would have to re-take the course in order to meet all educational requirements. Even though I could still graduate, in my mind I was not finished if I had to take this course a second time. But do you remember the second fact that I stated earlier? Not one student enrolled in this class had even an inkling of an idea of what our grades were even though numerous assignments had been submitted during this six-week course. Ten days had passed since our final exam and still <u>no</u> homework scores were received. Psychologically, I had prepared myself to another grueling six weeks during the next semester to repeat this one course. It felt as if the final grade of "66" had been engraved in my brain and I was very disappointed.

After over two grueling weeks which seemed like an eternity, our individual grades were finally being posted for all homework assignments that were submitted. One by one the grades came in. Six grades were posted for six weeks of submitted coursework. Much to my surprise, my study group had received perfect scores for all assignments submitted and as a result my final grade went from a "66" to a "99". Words could never explain the sheer joy and relief I felt as I stared at my computer screen. Our final score came from <u>all</u> the coursework submitted rather than the grade on one exam – which I had completely forgotten.

If you are asking what the moral of this story is, I'll tell you right now. This story is in NO WAY about intellect, hard work, team work, determination, or diligent efforts. Do you remember one important fact that was stated previously? It was important to me and my study group to maintain honesty and integrity in taking this final exam which meant taking it alone, without help or input from anyone even though our course leader would <u>never</u> had known the difference.

So many times we think that the things we do go unnoticed and in many cases that may be true. But no matter what we do, there will always be at least two people who know - you and God. God sees our heart and knows our motives even if our true motivations are unknown to us. At the heart of one's motives is what lies in the heart of each one of us. Decisions made, both good and bad, stem from our life experiences and the lessons we've learned along the way. Whether our actions are right or whether our actions are wrong, God sees and knows all. God never fails and neither will we as long as we live to honor Him.

Life does indeed throw us many "pop quizzes" but our morals and values are never tested as a group or team. But <u>being</u> tested is not the issue – what determines the outcome of life's tests depends on <u>how</u> we choose to take them. When it is all said and done, our final grade does not depend on one test alone but rather on an accumulation of trials and tribulations endured. Tests in school are administered to determine if we can actually apply what we have learned in a classroom; tests in life are endured to examine our faith because without tests, then there can be no _testimonies_...

Blessed is the one who perseveres under trial because, having stood the test, that person will receive the crown of life that the Lord has promised to those who love him (James 1:12)

Because you know that the testing of your faith produces perseverance. (James 1:3)

*Just remember that the most important gift you
can give to God is yourself...*

DAY TWELVE

GIFT WRAPPED

Everyone loves beautifully wrapped packages. The more beautifully a gift is wrapped, the more attention is drawn to the package and immediately you wonder what's inside the box. When we are handed a box that is gift wrapped, we usually smile with anticipation. Sheer excitement causes us to tear away the wrapping to hurriedly discover the contents of the box.

When you think about it you may realize that the gift wrapping is about sparking anticipation and surprise. Its sole purpose is to spark your interest to what's inside. The packaging gives no clues or insight as to what is to come.

We are all gift-wrapped boxes. You and I were gift wrapped by God. He wrapped each one of us in beautiful, distinctive wrapping. *We* are responsible for filling our box. An empty box has no purpose until it is filled.

Think about this...do you remember the last time you unwrapped a gift? What happened to the wrapping paper? Did you keep the wrapping or did you throw it away? Do you even remember *how* the gift was wrapped? No. The paper was torn away then thrown away. The only thing that's remembered is the gift itself.

When it's all said and done and God finally opens **your** box, what will He find inside? Will God see a reflection of Himself or will He find that your box was for decoration only? The answer to that question is totally up to you. Just remember that the most important gift you can give to God is yourself...

The very same God that created the heavens and the earth
is the same God that knows who you are.

DAY THIRTEEN

IMAGINE

According to the United States Census Bureau, the total world population is estimated to be approximately seven billion people. When I think of myself, compared to the rest of the billions of people on the planet, I am but a speck of sand of all the sand on a million beaches. What are the odds of one <u>specific</u> grain of sand being picked out of billions? Imagine seven billion people in one place at the same time, and your voice is heard over everyone else's. Imagine out of seven billion tickets distributed to every single person on earth, it is you who holds the winning ticket. Imagine the enormity of God taking the time to bless <u>you</u> out of billions of others.

One of the most fascinating accounts in the Bible is the story of Creation. Before Creation, the universe had no form, no substance, and no light. *(Genesis 1:2)* Then out of the words of God the universe was formed. *Then God said, "Let there be light," and there was light. (Genesis 1:3)* God then went on to create the sun, moon, stars, along with every living creature, including man.

In the days of Noah, the world had become so wicked and corrupt that God decided to destroy the entire human race along with all the animals of the earth and birds of the air (Genesis 6:7). But Noah found favor with God! Please stop and think about that statement – *Noah found favor with God.* Consider the total population during Noah's time. Imagine that, of all the people who had existed, God saw the righteousness of <u>one</u> man, Noah. Noah was a righteous man, the only blameless man on the earth at that time. (Genesis 6:9). God saw the heart of <u>one</u> man and as a result spared the human race from total destruction.

Many times we may think that our prayers are not heard. We

may think that God is too busy to concern Himself with what concerns us. There are times when we may get impatient because God is "taking too long" to answer our prayers. But we only have to look at God's "track record" to know that the same God who knew the heart of Noah is the same God who knows your heart and mine. We, as children of God, have access to the Creator of the universe. The same God that spoke directly to Moses also speaks to you and me. The same God that delivered Daniel out of the lion's den also delivers us from hurt, harm, and danger. The same God that can calm the sea with the sound of his voice is the same God that can quell whatever storms we face.

If we can hear birds sing, if we can feel a gentle breeze, if we can see one tiny ant crawling on a picnic table, then we can hear God, feel God, see God. The very same God that created the heavens and the earth is the same God that knows who you are. God has not changed and His love has not diminished with the passage of time. Out of approximately, seven billion people on the face of this Earth, God can still hear you, love you and bless you. *Imagine* what a great God we serve.

Since God is faithful and trustworthy,
then we are capable of the same.

DAY FOURTEEN

IN HIS OWN IMAGE

At one time or another, we have all had phone conversations with someone we have never seen. Somehow our mind sets an image of how that person may look. Somehow our psyche tries to match a face with the voice on the other end.

In my mind, I have a picture of what God looks like. I imagine Him being tall with unmistakable strength. I visualize a jovial disposition and eyes that show unimaginable, incredible love. I picture children making God laugh with the beauty of their innocence. I try not to imagine God just sitting on a throne, but rather God engaging and interacting like a loving Father spending quality time with His children.

An image is a reproduction of a person or thing or an exact likeness or semblance. Genesis 1:27 states that *man was created in the image of God*. This means that God created male and female to resemble Himself. Whenever I read this, the first thought that comes to my mind is the physical attributes of God, that I physically resemble the One who created me. But we all know that there is so much more to a person than their physical attributes. Personality, character, and demeanor all define the totality of who we are.

Since we were made in the exact image of God, then we should also possess His character and His Spirit. This means that since God is love, then we also have an amazing capacity to love. Because He is a forgiving God, then we too have the power to forgive. Since God is faithful and trustworthy, then we are capable of the same.

God fashioned male and female in His likeness. Because we were all created in His own image, as we take a look at ourselves, the person in the mirror should be a reflection of God Himself. He gave us the gift of His love so that we could love ourselves and love others. He forgives each one of us so that we can forgive our neighbors. Since God is the very essence of all that is good, all that is kind, all that is loving...then so are you!

So many times we put emphasis on the wrong thing.
We strive for convenience or the easy way.

DAY FIFTEEN

INCONVENIENCE

At one time I thought about changing churches. It wasn't because I was not being spiritually fed nor was it because I did not enjoy the worship service. The sole reason I was contemplating a change was because of the driving distance from my house to church, it was due to inconvenience.

The church I thought about attending is about five miles from home – very convenient on an early Sunday morning. During my contemplation, God asked me, "What is the longest daily distance you've ever driven to work?" "Thirty-five miles...each way," was my response to Him. Then God asked me, "How far is your *weekly* drive to church?" "Thirty miles...each way," was my answer. Then God asked me one final question, "What is more important?" My only appropriate response was, "Okay, Lord. I'm sorry."

If I can drive 70 miles on a *daily* basis, then how can 60 miles *weekly* be "inconvenient"? If you factor in the extremely heavy traffic during my daily work commute, then my weekly commute to church with absolutely no traffic to contend with could be considered a "cake walk". There was just no comparison! Hanging my head in shame, I had to ask myself the following questions: Who blessed me with transportation? GOD. Who blessed me with the money to put gas in my car? GOD. Who blessed me with the ability to even drive my car? GOD. So what should my priority be? *GOD.*

God has never put our prayers on hold just because He was busy blessing someone else. Out of approximately seven billion people on earth, God still has time to talk, to listen, to comfort. God always has time for us therefore we must make time to spend with Him.

Regardless of where I choose to worship my Lord and Savior, the odometer in my car will not be a determining factor. Just as God is never inconvenienced when He listens to our prayers, when He guides us in the direction in which we should go, or when He chooses to bless us, how can we contemplate mileage when paying homage to Him! The God we serve is worth the time and the distance…and He is definitely worth the "inconvenience".

*How different the world would be this very day if
Sarah had not taken God's promise into her own hands.*

DAY SIXTEEN

ISHMAEL OR ISAAC

Thousands of years ago, God made a promise to Abraham and his wife, Sarah. He promised that they would have a son. Sarah laughed at God's promise because of their ages and her infertility. Abraham was around 86 years old and Sarah was 76 when God's promise was made.

Sarah, in a state of disbelief, decided to "help" God fulfill His promise. She gave her maidservant, Hagar, to Abraham to bear a child. The plan was for Sarah and Abraham to raise the child as their own. In those days it was customary for a barren wife to raise the child of the wife's slave and her husband, as if the wife had given birth to the child.

When Ishmael was born to Abraham and Hagar, Sarah and Abraham became reconciled to the fact that God's promise of a son was fulfilled. But soon after the birth of Ishmael, Hagar began to feel superior to Sarah. Jealousy, mistrust and dislike between the two women grew, creating a predicament for Abraham. Who did Sarah blame? She blamed Abraham even though the strain and strife was a product of her very own idea.

Fourteen years later, Abraham and Sarah had a son. Abraham was 100 years old and Sarah was 90. God's promise was made manifest through Isaac. Isaac was the son of a promise and a covenant.

Hagar disliked Sarah, Sarah disliked Hagar and Ishmael, and Ishmael disliked his brother, Isaac. Upon Sarah's urging, Abraham banished Hagar and her son, Ishmael to the wilderness. Ishmael became a warrior and a hunter, he became wild and wayward. Ishmael had 12 sons and the tribes of Ishmael spread from Egypt to present-day Iraq.

But God's covenant was through Isaac not Ishmael. The covenant between God and Abraham was made *before* the birth of Ishmael. Isaac is the patriarch of Jacob, Joseph, and the Jews. Both the Jews and the Arabs are descendants of Abraham.

The purpose of this devotional is not a lesson in Bible history. It's a lesson on what can happen when we take the plans and promises of God and mold them into our own finite and limited way of thinking. It's about us making things happen instead of waiting on God. It's about God's timing, not ours.

How different the world would be this very day if Sarah had not taken God's promise into her own hands. If she had just trusted God's Word and waited for the manifestation of His promise, the history of mankind might be totally different. How many wars have been fought? How many lives have been lost? Thousands of years have passed and the repercussions of Sarah's "bright idea" are still being felt today. Sarah is blamed for the banishment of Hagar and Ishmael, the mother and son of the Arab nations. To this very day the conflict continues.

Even though Sarah decided to speed up God's plan, did God break His promise to Abraham? No. God still kept His promise and He blessed *both* sons of Abraham even though His covenant was with only one.

God has a plan, a purpose, and a promise for your life and mine. It's a plan that God decided before He knit us together in our mother's womb. When God gives you a purpose and promise it is up to God to make it happen and it is up to you to *let* it happen through faith and obedience. God does not need our help. Hold God to His word, and make sure that He can hold you to yours. Trying to figure it out on your own just may result in either an "Isaac" (The Promise) or an "Ishmael" (The Predicament).

Running on empty for too long can only result in depletion, yet it is at our weakest moments that God's grace can fill us back up.

DAY SEVENTEEN

RUNNING ON EMPTY

What do you do when you've done all you can do? What more can you give when you've given all you can give? How about feeling like you have absolutely no more to give? How is it that we even let ourselves get to that point?

Let me give you a quick analogy. Ever since I have owned my own car, I have made it a habit to not let the gas tank reach below a quarter of a tank. In my mind, that is when my gas tank needs to be filled back to a full tank. Once my car is refueled, I can drive it until the next time the gas gauge indicates that fuel is running low. But my point is this: Why will I make absolutely sure that the fuel in my car never reaches "empty", yet when it comes to MY tank, I let it go PAST empty? There are times when I will push myself beyond my limits, until I am actually "sputtering", running out of "gas". I seem to think that I can do just one more thing, achieve just one more task, or give just give a little bit more. But the reality is that sometimes I just cannot!

I had to begin to ask myself some questions. I started to ask myself what is it that I am really trying to do. To what place am I really trying to get? Who is it that I am really trying to reach? I was unable to answer ANY of these questions. Finally, I began to take this issue to God. I had to pray about it and really seek an answer from Him. Once I started to seek Him I realized that it was God who was asking me these questions. Still I had no answers...until now.

When Christ died on the cross, salvation was within our reach the moment we accepted Jesus as our Lord and Savior. But that can only mean one thing: It is not up us to save anyone and it is not up to us to save ourselves. God paid the ultimate price to secure our salvation by sending His Son to die for the forgiveness of our sins.

There comes a time when we must step out of God's way and let God be God. His giving has no limits and His motives are always pure. God has no need to depend on us, yet it is us who must depend on Him. Even with the best intentions and sincerity of heart, we must realize that even our giving may be flawed if we don't seek Him first. Running on empty for too long can only result in depletion, yet it is at our weakest moments that God's grace can fill us back up. Only then can we give to others as God gives to us – with a heart of love, in great abundance, and _never_ running on empty.

The moment that Jesus died on the Cross was the moment the penalty of sin was marked "paid in full" thereby cancelling a debt that we could never have paid on our own.

DAY EIGHTEEN

IT IS FINISHED

I remember being in graduate school for over two years when I completed the last requirement of my last course and received my last grade. I breathed a huge sigh of relief in knowing that a long journey had been completed and a new journey was about to begin. Once all the academic requirements were met I knew there was only one thing left for me to do and that was to accept my diploma as a "certificate of completion". I was finished!

Many of us have experienced the exact same thing – the completion of a long academic journey or certification process and the feeling of relief knowing that "it is finished". Once you're done, you're done – no one can come back and say that an error was made and you need to take one more course, read one more book, or pass one more test for your diploma or certificate of completion to be valid. *And so it is with the Cross.*

I remember when I watched *The Passion of Christ* for the first time. For the entire length of the film, it was extremely difficult for me to watch the cruelty and brutality inflicted on a totally innocent man, who knew no sin, yet willingly endured massive suffering for our salvation. Numerous times I thought of changing the channel but I resisted and watched the film from beginning to end so that I could gain a better perspective on what Christ endured for each one of us. Towards the end of the film while Jesus hung on the Cross, He asked for something to drink. After He had received the drink, Jesus uttered three words, "*It is finished!*" Jesus then bowed His head and gave up His spirit (John 19:30).

The moment that Jesus died on the Cross was the moment the penalty of sin was marked "paid in full" thereby cancelling a debt that we could never have paid on our own. The Cross is salvation's "certificate of completion" and all we have to do is receive it. No other requirements, obligations, or conditions are necessary. Think of it this way - How many of you, after paying off a debt and making the final payment, will then check to see if there is still a balance due? Once the debt is paid in full, there are no further payments necessary – you then receive written notification that your financial obligation has been cancelled. Your payment requirements are finished and freedom from that particular debt ensues. *And so it is with the Cross.*

There is One Man who hung, bled, and died for your sins and mine. There is One Man who was, is, and is to come again. There is One Man who is a spiritual representation of a sin debt that has been cancelled! When we accept the life, death, and resurrection of Christ – *IT IS FINISHED* – and our new journey in freedom begins... *(John 8:36; Galatians 5:1)*

When you feel bogged down with duties and obligations
along with an endless list of things to do – It's already done.

DAY NINETEEN

IT'S ALREADY DONE

I remember a time when I was really struggling. I was working full time and going to school. It's an understatement to say that I was stressed and overwhelmed with endless deadlines, duties, and responsibilities. There were times of real fear that I could not possibly fulfill all of my obligations.

So there I was, sitting in my church one Sunday morning yet again preoccupied with thinking about all the homework I had to do once I got home. My attention turned to the person preaching the sermon yet I had the nerve to be disappointed that it was a guest speaker! My mind kept going back and forth between duties and disappointment. Then I remember hearing from the pulpit just three simple words: "It's already done". Then I asked myself: "What's already done? What is this preacher talking about?"

What was being taught from the pulpit was what God wanted me to hear. I began to realize that when you feel bogged down with duties and obligations along with an endless list of things to do, there is no need to fret because *it's already done*. When you're looking for a job, but opportunities seem to come and go - *It's already done*. When your marriage is in turmoil and you cannot wait to get your relationship back on track - *It's already done*.

But what does <u>that</u> mean? It means that in God's eyes, all that we hope for is already provided. All that we struggle about has been resolved. All that we've prayed for has been answered. God's time is past, present, and future. Eternity past and eternity future are one and the same to Him. Our present is God's past. And although God is ever-present with us, He is infinitely beyond where we are.

At the end of the church service, I felt comforted knowing that the homework I had to do when I got home was already done – in the eyes of God. The pressure I felt was gone – in God's eyes. And although I had not yet lived it, it already existed in God's past.

Take a brief moment to think about something that may be heavy on your heart. Think about the job that seems unattainable. Think about the burdens that seem to wear you down. But then KNOW that God has already comforted your heart, blessed you with that great new job, totally lifted that burden. It's DONE! In God's time, your problems will meet your solutions; your questions will meet your answers. It takes faith to lay your burdens before the Lord. But know that God's past will coincide with your present. It's only a matter of God's time - until it's done…

It is through the articulation of emotions that convey the soul.

DAY TWENTY

JUST SAY IT

Whether a death is sudden, accidental or somewhat expected has no bearing on one's feelings of sadness and loss. The age of a deceased friend or loved one is likewise not a determinant in one's anguish.

One day, I was attending a funeral and suddenly I realized what truly matters in life. I found myself thinking of my family and friends. Then for a brief second I thought of my job. Next thing that came to mind were a few issues that I had been dealing with that instantly seemed miniscule and unimportant. In my mind and in my heart, I thought of how blessed I had been to know the person of whose memorial I was attending.

I attended a memorial of a very spirit-filled Christian woman who was like an aunt to me since high school. She was actually the aunt of my very best friend. I was awesomely touched to see how many people were in attendance. Not surprisingly, she was loved by many more people than by just me.

The week before she went to heaven, I went to visit her. Her smile as I entered the room made the sun seem dim by comparison. Her smile was confirmation of God's grace and loving kindness. At the end of my visit, I did not realize that I would call her "Auntie" for the very last time. Before I left I told her that I loved her. Her responsive smile was evidence of her love for me as well.

So many times we love in silence. How many times do we pass up perfect opportunities to tell someone we love them? We all know how the saying goes: "Action speaks louder than words". But there may actually be times when this is not the case. Sometimes just hearing the words, "I love you", can mean so much.

Can you imagine children never hearing those words from their parents? How about never hearing those words from a spouse? Sometimes those three words can mean more than a gift bought from a department store. Sometimes those three words can say so much more than a card or even a poem.

A dear friend once reminded me of one of the biggest mistakes I have ever made. It's a mistake that I promised myself that I would never repeat. It was my unwillingness to "just say it"…to just say three little words to someone I truly cared about. I had not taken into account that it is God who reads the heart but it is people who hear the words. Merely thinking of your love for someone does not impart your feelings. It is through the articulation of emotions that convey the soul. Love that is expressed is love that is shared.

If you love, show it. If you love, feel it. If you love, *JUST SAY IT*. Don't make the mistake of not letting those three little words escape your lips. Say it while you have the opportunity and bask in the bliss when "I love you" is said back to you. Saying those three little words just may be the biggest mistake that you will *never* make…

*At the very moment anxiety strikes us,
we are to turn our focus to God.*

DAY TWENTY-ONE

A LESSON LEARNED

I learned a very valuable lesson while going to school and working full-time. I was stressed out at work while school was very difficult and demanding. There were projects at work that had to be completed as well as deadlines for school that had to be met.

To say that I felt overwhelmed was an understatement. Many times I prayed and had long talks with God about how I was feeling. Each time I prayed God gave me one word and one word only: *"focus"*. Soon I began to reflect on that one word. On my way to work one morning, I was listening to a famous preacher on the radio. While he was speaking about unshakeable peace, he mentioned the word, "focus". He stated that at the very moment anxiety strikes us, we are to turn our focus to God.

Right then I knew that God was confirming what He had told me several times before. I realized that my focus was nowhere on God, but rather on how I was feeling. I had lost by center point, which meant that I had no balance. The scales were tipped in the wrong direction. Only with God as my focal point could the scales be tipped in my favor.

Soon my prayers were totally different. I thought about the stress at work and thanked God for my job. I remember contemplating the long chapters that had to be read and the homework that had to be done for the class I was taking at that time. But then I thanked God for the opportunity to go to school. I focused on all that God had brought me through in the past instead of what I was going through right then. My focus was no longer on the long months of working and going to school that I thought would never end. My focus was on

God, my one and only true source of unshakeable peace

Even though the conditions in my life are different now, my focus must remain the same. It is so easy to get caught up in things that must be done rather than on the blessing of being able to get things done in the first place. I find myself continually trying to remember that in order to change my attitude or circumstances, I must first change my focus. Sometimes it may be as simple as finding *just one reason* to thank God even during the tough times.

God, in all of His gentleness and patience, taught me a lesson using only one word, "Focus". Focusing on life's disappointments, stress, or anxiety distracts us from what is really important which is placing God front and center while placing life's challenges on the back burner. Keeping our focus on Him gives us a sense of balance and gives us peace. It is a lesson learned that I hope to never forget.

You will keep in perfect peace all who trust in you, whose thoughts are fixed on you! (Isaiah 26:3)

The Cross is our only source of light in a dark world because the light of Christ illumines the soul.

DAY TWENTY-TWO

LET THERE BE LIGHT

I once worked in an office building where the light in each individual office would turn on automatically as soon as someone walked in. When an office was empty for a certain period of time, the light would automatically turn off. When I sat and thought about this, a "light" came on in my head (yes, pun intended)!

There are times when we enter a room and there is no light. In a room of unbelievers the light is non-existent. When we, as children of God, enter the scene the light automatically comes on because Jesus is now on the scene and we are a reflection of His light. When God created the universe one of the very first things He did was separate the light from the darkness by creating the sun, the moon and the stars. The moment we accept Christ, we immediately move from the darkness of night into the light of day.

Can you imagine a world shrouded in complete darkness, void of any semblance of light? In the Book of Revelation during the time of the Great Tribulation, it states that God will send a judgment in which the entire earth will be cast into complete darkness. *(Revelation 16:10)* This darkness will not be the equivalent of losing electrical power or the sun not rising, but rather a blackness that is so palpable that a person will be able to actually feel the absence of light. There will be not one single source of light on the face of the earth. This supernatural nightfall will be inescapable. This darkness will be a forecast of the eternity to be suffered by all who willfully reject Christ and representative of the true character of a hardened heart.

Prior to this judgment of God, the Bible states that all believers in Christ will be caught up and taken to be with the Lord forever. *(1 Thessalonians 4:16-17)*. The moment that believers in Christ are removed, then the world will consist of only non-believers. If God considers Christians to be the light of the world *(Matthew 5:14)*, then a world without Christians is a world automatically situated in darkness!

Right now, there are certain parts of the earth that experience "polar nights" where there is no sunshine for months at a time. During this time, research has proven that people are more prone to depression, insomnia, anxiety and a host of other effects on the human psyche. But even during polar nights, "artificial" light can be generated through electricity or some other external power source – not so during the time of the righteous judgment of God as described in the Book of Revelation.

If you are wondering what's my point, then here it is: No matter how bright the sun shines, no matter the number of light switches or light bulbs, apart from God there is NO LIGHT!!! The Cross is our only source of light in a dark world because the light of Christ illumines the soul. When God separated the day from the night, not only did He separate the light from the darkness, but He also called us into the light of Christ, forever calling us into Himself.

You are the light in a dark room and that light is Jesus Christ – now go forth and let it shine…

Then God said, "Let there be light," and there was light. God saw that the light was good, and he separated the light from the darkness. (Genesis 1:3-4)

Which voice is more clear, your friend's or your foe's?

DAY TWENTY-THREE

LOOK WHO'S TALKING

During a conversation with a friend, a statement was made that caught my attention. He stated that Satan never talks to him, that he never hears from the enemy. What surprised me even more than the statement was the fact that he was not joking, he was very serious. As we discussed it a bit further, I told him that I regularly hear from the enemy as well as from God. He was surprised by my statement as well.

A few days later this particular conversation came to mind. I prayed for my friend because I knew that he was in a "danger zone". As I prayed, God made me see that if one cannot recognize the voice of Satan, then surely one cannot recognize the voice of God. Now when I hear or feel something in my spirit I try to remember to **look at who's talking** to me. I have to ask myself if it's from God or from the adversary.

Deception is a primary tool used by Satan. To believe that he does not exist or is not an active part of your life is trickery and very dangerous. A battle cannot be fought nor won if your enemy is unknown. Have you ever seen a soldier fight while blindfolded? The key to victory is to know who and what you're fighting, why you're fighting and you *must* believe that you can win the war. A war that cannot be won should never be fought.

As I thought about this I remembered one fact that I so often forget. The battle was fought when Jesus died on the cross. The war was won when He rose from the dead. The moment we accepted Christ was the very moment we became victors, we became members of the winning team.

Our victory in the battle of life does not mean that the enemy has disappeared. Being victorious in no way means that you let down your guard. The war has already been won but we all still battle conflict, antagonism, and temptation on a daily basis. We are in active communication with a defeated foe, Satan, as well as a triumphant friend, Christ. Which voice is more clear, your friend's or your foe's? It is up to us to decipher and know the difference, it is up to us to... *"look who's talking"*!

Love is meant to be shared, not contained.

DAY TWENTY-FOUR

LOVE IN ACTION

There are few topics that excite me more than the topic of love. Usually when I think of the word, "love", I think of it as a noun - the **love** I have for someone or the **love** of God. What I want to focus on right now is "love" as a verb, an *action* word.

Love that is stagnant is love that does not move, it just sits there with nothing to do. When you take love and put it into action then love spreads and flourishes. Love is meant to be shared, not contained.

Love in action is not a difficult concept. It's actually quite simple. Love in action is hugging a friend that's down and out or a father and son throwing a baseball in the back yard. It's answering the phone in the middle of the night and listening to a friend pour out their heart in despair. Love in action is buying a newspaper from the man on the corner rather than buying one from a supermarket just so that man can reap the benefit. Simple acts of kindness are huge displays of love.

During my prayer time, I try to remember to always tell God how much I love Him. But it was during a particularly hectic time in my life with the demands of balancing work and school that I focused on how much God loves me, how much He loves each one of us. I thought about how God put *His* love into action. I visualized the Cross. I envisioned the nails being pounded into the hands and feet of Jesus. I saw the crown of thorns and the blood of Christ dripping from His face. All His pain, all His suffering was love in **action**.

There is nothing we could ever do that could even come close to the sacrifice that Christ made for us. But all He asks of us is to love. Love is so vital and so necessary to who we are in Christ.

To feel loved is a blessing, but to **give** love is a command from God. Love given from the heart is love received in the soul. Put love into action and watch love come right back to you. Use love as a verb, an **action** word, and love will manifest in your life as a noun.

Miracles may be the most unpredictable events
in the course of time

DAY TWENTY-FIVE

MIRACLES

Most often when one thinks of a miracle, we think of grand gestures performed by God. The parting of the Red Sea may come to mind. You may also be reminded of the burning bush seen by Moses. Jesus raising the dead and healing the sick are also manifestations of the miracles of God. A miracle is defined as, "*an event that appears inexplicable by the laws of nature and so is held to be supernatural in origin or an act of God.*"

But what about the everyday miracles that we often do not recognize? Remember the time when a friend just happened to call you at one of your weakest moments? How amazing it was that they thought of you at the very moment you needed them the most. Their words of encouragement stopped your tears that flowed right before you answered their call. What about a day you were unusually late for work? While driving to work on the freeway you noticed a terrible car accident. Ever thought your car could have been involved in that specific accident but God spared you by running behind schedule? Fifteen minutes earlier could have changed your life with devastating consequences.

There are many miracles that live and breathe every day. Miracles may not only be extraordinary circumstances but can also be the person sitting next to you on a city bus. What about the baby that was born mortally ill but God spared the life of that child? What about the parents who were told by doctors that their tiny infant would be mentally incapacitated but God said, "No way – that's _MY_ child?"

One Sunday morning, God sent me my very own miracle. My miracle sat next to me in church on an unusually difficult day. It was a sunny day, but I didn't notice. There were no clouds in the sky, but it felt as if a cloud hung over my head. The choir sang and my tears started to flow. A perfect stranger lent me their shoulder and right then I felt His presence – it was the presence of God Himself. As my head rested on their shoulder I felt as if God were holding me in His arms, it felt like Home. Right then I thanked God for sending me an angel – for sending me a tiny miracle on an ordinary Sunday morning.

To this very day I still thank God for that particular miracle. It was the miracle of a new friendship with an angel that God sent my way. It was the miracle of hearing God say that He loves me through a simple hug and a sincere smile from a perfect stranger.

One never knows how God will bring joy in times of sadness or comfort in times of distress. Miracles may be the most unpredictable events in the course of time. One day a perfect stranger may look into your eyes and _you_ could very well be that person's miracle, their angel sent to them by God. There are times that God will use us to be an angel to those in need through a sincere hug, a kind word, or a simple smile. How do I know? I know because the angel that God sent to me that ordinary Sunday morning is now my friend.

...there is only one source of truth, love, peace and forgiveness on which we can all stand – the Word of God.

DAY TWENTY-SIX

ONE SOURCE

We are living in the information age. Facts and figures can be obtained with the click of a computer mouse and a few strokes on a keyboard. Books, newspapers, and magazines are just a few sources of information.

Despite all the different avenues that may be traveled in our quest for knowledge, there is but *one source* of absolute truth – the Word of God. The Bible is the sole foundation for everyday living. The Word of God is an encyclopedia on the history of mankind – past, present, and future. It is a dictionary that defines the meaning of life. It is a cookbook filled with recipes for success.

We live in a world in which everything changes, nothing stays the same. People change and circumstances change. There are no two days exactly alike because the world is in a constant state of flux and instability. But God's Word is unchangeable, it is pure and unadulterated.

What other book besides the Bible can convict the sinner and at the same time offer comfort and hope for the convicted? What other source of truth can change the heart of a man and at the same time reveal the heart of God? God, in all His glory, did not put us in a "sink or swim" situation. Instead He gave us rules and guidelines that withstand the test of time.

The Bible tells us that we are all sinners who fall short of the glory of God. But God's Word is feared by sinners nonetheless. Ironically, it is fear of condemnation and fear of conviction that deters our seeking of knowledge and truth. Fear of God's Word can hold us in bondage and enslave us. Yes, the Word does convict us of our sins but it never condemns those who belong to Christ *(Romans 8:1)*.

For all our doubts, fears, anxieties and uncertainties, there is only *one source* of truth, love, peace and forgiveness on which we can all stand – the Word of God. It reveals who we are and who God is. In a world of no absolutes, the Word of God is our *one source* of absolute power and timeless truth for eternity past and eternity future. To know God is to know His Word...

*Talk to God like He's your very best friend
because in reality that is exactly what He is...*

DAY TWENTY-SEVEN

OPEN CONVERSATION

I have always admired those who are able to pray out loud in a structured setting. There are those who can effortlessly pray aloud before scores of others. Structured prayer is very difficult for me.

The moment I begin to pray is the very moment I get into "conversation mode". If you were ever able to see me praying while driving my car, you would probably deem me certifiable. It would look as if I am talking to myself behind the wheel of my car. If you were to ever see me praying at home, you would be prone to think I was talking to the air we breathe.

Prayer is open communication with God. I call prayer, "conversation with God." I converse with Him just like I would talk to my best friend. Many times I find myself just telling Him my thoughts and feelings as if He were sitting in a chair facing me. But in all reality, that is exactly where God is…right before me listening to my prayerful conversation with Him. Sometimes I find myself starting with this phrase, "OK God, I know you already know this but I'll tell you anyway!" Then I tell Him what is on my mind and in my heart.

To humbly confess and openly profess to God allows intimacy in your relationship with Him. You cannot surprise Him because He knows all. You cannot hide from Him because He sees all. To openly converse with Him is to lay prostrate at His feet. It equates to allowing God into your spirit while removing the clutter that may clog your mind.

You can pray to God anytime and anywhere, but find a place where you can talk to Him freely. Find a spot where you can openly engage in conversation with God that is comfortable, quiet, and familiar. Let your "prayer spot" be a place where you can pour out your heart to God while He pours out His love to you.

Open conversations with God may not be structured prayers but rather open dialogue. Prayer is an open exchange and it is reciprocal. Talking to God opens the door for God to speak to you. Taking time to listen to your heart is the same as listening to the heart of God. How wonderful it is to know that the Creator of the universe takes time to spend with you. How comforting it is to know that you have a loving Father who is always willing to listen to His children.

God is never too busy to hear from us. He is never too distracted to bless us. He is never unavailable. Talk to God like He's your very best friend because in reality that is exactly what He is - a loving, trustworthy, friend with whom we can at any time engage in *open conversation.*

The posture of your heart will
definitely determine the posture of your body.

DAY TWENTY-EIGHT

POSTURE

Most people think of posture as the position of the body. Sitting, standing, kneeling, laying are all body postures. Have you ever thought about the *posture of your heart*? What *is* the posture of your heart?

Ask yourself these questions: What do you stand up for? Do you just sit back and let the world pass you by? Would you lay down your life for a friend? Do you only kneel in prayer when troubles come?

The manifestation of a heavy heart will show in body posture. Someone with a troubled soul may have problems walking tall or sitting straight. Someone facing depression may lay all day with no motivation to get up and get going. What is in your heart is the key to how you live your daily life. The posture of your heart will definitely determine the posture of your body. Your internal state of being will be manifested externally.

What's your heart position and soul condition? Take this day to search your heart. Take a stand for what's right. Don't' just sit back and let the world determine who you are. Lay down your burdens before God. Kneel before the Creator of your heart in praise and thanksgiving.

The only heart we can change is our own. A heart that stands tall is a heart that God can use. Again I ask: What is the posture of your heart?

The logic of man is no match for the Spirit of God.

DAY TWENTY-NINE

THE ADAM AND EVE SYNDROME

Have you ever wondered what it was like in the Garden of Eden? I can bet that we each have our own mental picture of what the Garden was like – trees in abundance, flowers in bloom, perfect green grass, and exceptionally wonderful weather. The Bible states that water came from out of the ground and watered all the land (Genesis 2:6). The earth had its own natural sprinkler system; true paradise existed on the earth.

When man was created, God placed Adam in the Garden. Adam had food to eat and water to drink. Adam could eat from _any_ tree in the entire garden except one – the tree of the knowledge of good and evil. Let me stop here for a minute to repeat just one fact – Adam could eat from ANY tree. Isn't it just like God to give us not only what we need, but <u>more</u> than we need! And isn't it just like man to focus on what we cannot have rather than what we do have! This is what I call the "Adam and Eve Syndrome" – the propensity to focus on what we do <u>not</u> have rather than on what we do.

Let me give you an example of this "syndrome". As long as I have had knowledge of God's Word, I have known about the concept of giving back to God what is God's. God says that we are to give one tenth of our increase. When we think of this command we usually think of what we are to give rather than on the gift that remains. God allows us to retain ninety percent of what He gives to us – ninety percent! It's almost synonymous with seeing a glass half empty or half full. Adam and Eve could eat from any tree in the garden ("glass half full"), except from one tree they could not eat ("glass half empty"). Now think of what the state of humanity would be like today if they had not focused on that one tree.

The "syndrome" causes us to focus on the minor portion that we are to give rather than the major portion that remains. Maybe this concept may cause reluctance because we think we can do more with <u>all</u> God has given us rather than with only a portion of it. Logically you may think this to be true, but this concept is not based on logic. God even says that we can test Him and watch it come to pass. The logic of man is no match for the Spirit of God.

Please let me make it clear that my main focus is not on the concept of tithing because we all know what God says about it, but rather, it's to point out the generosity of the God we serve. So many times we are blessed by God and we just cannot see the blessings because our focus is elsewhere. If our blessings look different than what we expect, we don't see it. If our blessings don't sound familiar, we don't hear it. In the Garden, God provided everything that man needed with only one exception, but it was that one exception that became the rule.

God walked in the Garden of Eden (Genesis 3:8) and communed with man. Adam had direct access to God until his focus changed. Adam and Eve's concentration on one forbidden tree resulted in their inability to eat from countless others in the Garden and caused a barrier with their communion with God, but the story did not end there. Just as sin entered into the world through one man, Adam, life was restored through one man, Jesus (Romans 5:15). It is through Christ that our communion with God was restored and we are ever victorious over the "Adam and Eve Syndrome".

The world is full of givers and takers, but being one
who receives is quite different...

DAY THIRTY

RECEIVE

We all know how the saying goes: "It's better to give than to receive". Yes, I do agree with this statement but there are times when one must learn how to receive.

The world is full of givers and takers, but being one who receives is quite different. There are those who give regularly of themselves with no expectations of anything in return. A giver may lend a shoulder to cry on but may have trouble crying on someone else's shoulder. They may be quick to wipe the tears of a loved one but very hesitant to show their silent tears. They can forgive others more readily than they can forgive themselves.

How many times have you begged God for forgiveness over and over again? God says that when we ask for forgiveness, He remembers our sins no more. In reality, we are repeatedly asking God to pardon us for something that He has already forgotten. His mercy is freely given but reluctantly received. The only thing left to do is to forgive ourselves.

The ability to love and love freely is truly a gift, but the ability to **receive** love in return is equally important. Emotional bankruptcy is a byproduct of the inability to receive. Imagine a checking account where checks are only written but no funds are ever deposited. Without deposits there are no withdrawals. So it is with love – you must have a source from which to withdraw.

So many times in prayer, we often communicate our love for God. I find myself time and again reiterating my love to God. But there are not many times when I'll just sit back and focus on God's love for me. Heartfelt expressions to God may come natural but remembering *His* love is not the norm.

God is a God of love and loving Him is just as vital as letting Him love us. Learning to receive just might better enable you to give. Let your heart be full of love – love to be given but also love to be received. For a heart to grow, love must be given, but love most definitely must also be received. Receive love today so that you can give love tomorrow…

The very thing you fear is the very thing that could manifest in your life.

DAY THIRTY-ONE

FEAR NOT

Fear is defined as "an unpleasant feeling of anxiety or apprehension caused by the presence or anticipation of danger". It can also be defined as worry. There are other ways to define fear, but not one definition has a positive connotation as fear signifies angst and unease.

In the human sense, we may tend to think that some fear is justifiable, such as a fear of walking alone at night down an abandoned street. But this is actually common sense rather than fear! There are many situations that we avoid based on safety and security. Yet there are other instances in which fear is faith in reverse.

The Bible states that God does not give us a spirit of fear. Since God does not give us the spirit of fear, then who does? If fear is erratic faith, then the author of fear comes from the foe of God, Satan himself. The greatest fear that Satan inflicts on us is the fear that the promises of God will not come to pass.

One of the key things taught in risk management is that the one and only way to prevent a loss from occurring is to avoid an activity altogether, if possible. It makes perfect sense but only if we live in a perfect world! The only way to avoid an auto accident is not to drive a car, but how feasible is that? To avoid some risks may actually void a blessing.

I remember working on a job for twelve years with a company that I loved working for. I also remember being so content with that job that at one point I began to wonder (worry is more honest) about what would happen if I lost that job. I had just started school and was worried about how I could possibly finish my education with no job. But instead of rejecting the fear of unemployment, I accepted it and kept it. Yes, I always wanted to do a good job, but soon I was working harder to keep my job rather than to excel at it.

One morning while getting ready for work, I heard on the local news that the company I worked for was getting acquired by another company. The moment I sat in my office at my computer, the news was confirmed; we were getting bought out by another corporation. I became afraid that after working there for twelve years, year number thirteen was out of reach. The main situation that I feared was the exact thing that happened! Four months later I was unemployed. But that's not the end of the story. Getting laid off was a blessing in disguise because not only did God supply my needs financially, He also allowed me time off during my most difficult courses in school.

If you are wondering if I experienced fear of any kind during my unemployment, the answer is, "YES". But fear is the one place where I could not stay. I had to find where fear existed, face it, and then fight it. The only way I knew how to do that was to thank God for where I was, no matter the circumstance, then thank Him for where He was taking me. I thanked God for my new job every day even <u>while</u> I was searching for that new job.

Yes, there have been other times in my life that I have been stifled by fear and as much as I hate to admit it, those times are <u>not</u> indicative of me walking by faith. But fear that is not fought has a way of being self-fulfilling. The very thing you fear is the very thing that could manifest in your life. If God does not give us the "spirit" of fear, then any fear we face is of the "spirit" realm and must be fought by the Spirit of God.

I wish that I could honestly say that my life is totally absent of any fear, but that would be untruthful. But <u>tolerated</u> fear is representative of <u>tainted</u> faith. In order to combat fear, I <u>must</u> put God smack dab between me and that which I fear then stand behind Him as the battle is fought and the war is won. As long as I let God fight the battle, then I have nothing to fear…

God says, "Fear not, for I am with you…" (Isaiah 41:10)

*Sometimes we may have a sense of pride that
we may not even recognize. Often times
our dependence may be in our own principles rather
than on God's ability to lead and guide us.*

DAY THIRTY-TWO

SELF-RELIANCE

I once had a very humbling experience. It was one moment in time that made me realize just where my strength comes from. I was at a powerless point in a powerful position. It was something that I had prayed about for a while but realized that my prayer was not the most humble prayer.

A very wise woman once told me that even though we pray we must still rely on God for strength and guidance. She said that it is by God's *grace* that leads us on the right path, not by just prayer alone. She said that we must pray for the grace of God for direction instead of thinking that it is by our own will that spiritual battles are fought and won, not *self-reliance.*

Sometimes we may have a sense of pride that we may not even recognize. Often times our dependence may be in our own principles rather than on God's ability to lead and guide us. To rely on self rather than Spirit is not difficult to do but may be very difficult to recognize. Our prayer, our faith, and our strength must be based on what God can do *through* us and not on what we can do ourselves.

So many times I had prayed for the spirit of humility, for a humble heart. Now my prayer is just a little bit different. Yes, I still pray for a humble heart but now I also pray for God's grace to keep me from doing the things I should not do and to do the things I should. No longer can I rely on sheer willpower to fight my battles. Until I felt a sense of helplessness did I realize that the only power I have is in God and Him alone.

God can and will open the windows of heaven to bestow opportunities and blessings on His children. But *self-reliance* can open doors to pride that only He can close. The moment we recognize our powerlessness apart from Him is the moment we receive power that only He can give. It is at that moment that we are the strongest, it is at that moment that the battle is won...

It has been said that the shortest distance between two points is a straight line. Sometimes with God that is definitely not the case.

DAY THIRTY-THREE

STEPS

The need for safety and security are basic human necessities. We all strive to reach a level of contentment in where we are and what we do. Feelings of wellbeing may come as a result of languishing in comfort zones that we somehow unknowingly create.

But have you ever been in a position in which you are forced out of "hibernation"? What happens when you can no longer hide in the shadows of your zones of refuge? Have you ever felt a nudging in your heart that it is time to step out?

Picture yourself walking into a classroom. You immediately take the first available seat at the back of the classroom. You tend to blend in with the rest of the students so much so that rarely are you called on by the teacher. Feelings of ease result in knowing that you are hidden in the background.

Then one day the instructor walks to the back of the classroom into your place of immunity. You are caught completely off guard and are totally unprepared. You are then called upon for class participation. Instantly you are at the forefront, forced from your solemn sanctuary of silence.

Currently you may find yourself in a similar situation – pushed from the shadows. No longer can you hide nonchalantly basking in obscurity. God is in the process of having you step out so that you can step up. You now must move horizontally in order to vertically advance. Your comfort zones suddenly seem unavailable and out of reach.

Let me give you an example. It was while driving to church one Sunday morning that I finally got the picture. There was one specific prayer request that God emphatically just would not allow. No matter how I posed the question, the answer was still the same. I finally got to the point to where I actually had to concede. In the end it was my heart that needed to change, not God's. When at last I told God that I heartily accepted His decision, it was then that all was revealed. I was seeking security from an insecure source. God was trying to remove all the walls that existed in my life but my prayer request in reality was just another barrier. How easy it would be to hide behind another person, place, or thing rather than to just step out on faith. How easy it would be to fade into the backdrop of anonymity only to avoid specificity.

It has been said that the shortest distance between two points is a straight line. Sometimes with God that is definitely not the case. There are times when God must move you out (horizontally) in order for you to move up (vertically). Moving out of your comfort zones means moving forward in faith which equals moving up God's ladder to success. It is only then can you rest in God's comfort zone of victory, but it is up to you to take that first step.

With a simple kiss, a little boy with a mental disability taught me...
that love given freely, even to a perfect stranger, is a gift.

DAY THIRTY-FOUR

THE KISS

Sitting in church one Sunday morning, I noticed a little boy in the pew ahead of where I sat. He was around nine or ten years old with Down Syndrome. What struck me most about this little boy was his happy disposition. He danced to almost every song sang by the choir. He clapped and sang as best he could. As I watched him with utter amazement, I found that my heart became full and joyful. His cheerful countenance was like a breath of fresh air. Throughout the church service he smiled, laughed, clapped, sang, and danced.

When the little boy walked back from receiving Communion, I directed him back to his seat as he had passed up his pew. Suddenly and without hesitation he hugged me and kissed me on my right cheek. My heart smiled as he walked back to his seat. He never gave me a second glance nor a second thought. But right then and there his kiss on my right cheek helped me put things into perspective.

With a simple kiss, a little boy with a mental disability taught me what the smartest person on earth could probably not communicate. He taught me that love given freely, even to a perfect stranger, is a gift.

Many of us are very hesitant when it comes to demonstrating love. Fear of rejection often keeps us from showing simple acts of love to those who mean the most. Telling someone you love them can be done without the use of words or phrases. Sometimes a hug, a kiss, a smile will speak volumes as well as move mountains.

The night before this particular Sunday church service, for some unknown reason I thought of what I deem to be the most demonstrative display of adoration. To kiss the back of a woman's right hand to me is the utmost sign of respect and reverence. How long had it been since I had been shown such admiration? It had been so long that I could not remember.

At the end of the church service, this little boy exited his pew by walking to my end of the row. As I waved him good-bye he smiled and took the back of my right hand and kissed it. It was like a reflex for him to show such respect. It was like a reflex for me to stand frozen in awe.

As I said my prayers that night it finally dawned on me what two innocent kisses from one little boy signified. God used a little boy, an angel, to demonstrate God's love for me, for us. Just as this little boy's acts of tenderness and kindness were spontaneous and pure, God's love for us is the same – unscripted, unstructured, unplanned. His love is natural and given freely.

One Sunday morning, God gave me a hug, a kiss on my right cheek, and a kiss on the back of my right hand through an angel, a little boy with a happy heart. With such innocence, tenderness, and beauty, it's a kiss I'll always remember from a little boy I'll never forget…

Trust is something that must be earned
but never demanded.

DAY THIRTY-FIVE

TRUSTED

During a lifetime many situations arise in which we must let go and trust. Many times it is a family member or a friend in whom we may place our trust. Trust means to rely upon or place confidence in someone or something.

Trust is something that must be earned but never demanded. Whether we know it or not we are trusted by many different people in various situations and circumstances. When someone needs to hear the truth, you may be the one trusted to be honest. In times of despair, you may be the one trusted to lift one's spirits.

What you are trusted to bring into another person's life may depend on your personal track record as a friend or a loved one. Has anyone ever called you just to request a prayer from you? If so, it's because you can be trusted as a prayer partner. Has anyone ever come to you to pour out their heart in the strictest of confidence? If so, it's because you can be trusted as a confidant or a sounding board.

The ways and means in which you can be trusted may be a strong indication of one's character. What you are trusted to say and do may be indicative of how you are perceived by others. There are those who can only be trusted for fun and frivolity but never trusted for the gift of fellowship or a solid foundation of faith.

There is but one man in whom we can truly place our trust and that man is Jesus Christ. Only He can be trusted to never hurt us, to never disappoint us. Only He can be trusted to fill our needs.

God created each one of us for a specific purpose. He has a plan for your life and mine. The only question is: Can God trust us to make His plan come to pass...

There are times when knowing the truth is just not enough.

DAY THIRTY-SIX

THE TRUTH ABOUT TRUTH

How many of us have heard the phrase, "The truth will set you free"? I have heard this countless times and considered this statement to actually be the truth. But I have learned that this phrase in itself may not actually be accurate. During a Christian program it was stated that <u>knowing</u> the truth does not set you free. I was stunned by this statement and wanted to know what this statement meant. I listened further for an explanation.

We all know many things to be true. For example, we know that to lose weight, we must eat right and exercise. Yet just <u>knowing</u> this fact does not cause us to lose weight. It is only with the application of this truth will we see results.

Sure, there are numerous things we know to be true and there are truths we apply to our daily lives, but there is only <u>one</u> truth by which we can be saved and that is through the sacrificial death of our Lord, Jesus Christ. There is no question that the Bible, the Word of God, provides us with this truth. It is also true that God gives us the choice of whether or not we will believe it and accept it.

There are three things that I have learned from my journey with God. First, I have noticed that the more truth I sought, the more truth I found once I asked God to lead me to His truth. Second, I have noticed the more I learn, the more I want to know. Third, any knowledge I obtain can only be considered truth if it lines up with the Word of God – good news is not good news if it not biblically based.

There are times when knowing the truth is just not enough. Freedom comes from the application of truth and God's truth is the only truth that matters. But please don't just take my word for it, find out for yourself. Ask for God to reveal His truth to you. Test what you hear, examine what you read against God's Word which is without error. Know <u>His</u> truth, believe it, apply it – and His truth will set you free…

John 8:31-32 states, *"If you hold to my teaching, you are really my disciples. Then you will know the truth, and the truth will set you free."*

Many times God may allow us to endure
a wilderness experience not by His own choosing
but solely by our own actions.

DAY THIRTY-SEVEN

WILDERNESS EXPERIENCE

Remember the Israelites, God's chosen people? God promised them a land flowing with milk and honey. He vowed that they would inhabit the Promised Land. But before they reached their destination they wandered through the wilderness for 40 years as a result of their rebellion and disobedience against God. They underwent a "wilderness experience" of their own making.

Many times God may allow us to endure a *wilderness experience* not by His own choosing but solely by our own actions. So often we aimlessly wander as in a maze when the only path to take is a straight line—straight into the promises of God. Many times our trust in God is the only way out of "the wilderness".

I remember my own "wilderness experience". During this time I had lunch with a trusted friend, a prayer partner. Even though she had no idea of my struggles, her words of wisdom rang true. She said that we are to thank God even through our trials and we must pray our way through the tough times. The sincerity in her voice signified that she was not engaging in mere "pep talk". After lunch I thought about our conversation. It seemed as if her words were like little arrows God was using to lead me out of the "wilderness". Her words fed my spirit like the manna from Heaven that God sent to feed His chosen people while wandering through the wild.

Later that same day another trusted friend imparted wise words. He said that there are times when we may endure many burdens before receiving many blessings. He said that enduring hardships may just mean that you are living on the edge... living on the edge of a blessing from God. To jump too soon may mean forfeiture of God's fruit but to linger on the edge for too long may also mean blocked blessings.

While attending Church one Sunday morning I realized that I was actually looking *BACK* at my wilderness experience. The sermon topic was about praising God. It was then that I realized that I had made it through. It finally dawned on me that much stress and many frustrations had been clouding my vision. Prayer and praise were necessary to lead me out of a weary wasteland of aimless wandering. Until the fog was lifted from my eyes, I could not see the forest for the trees.

Right then I remembered that as I was driving to Church I was thinking and wondering why I had not heard God speak to me in quite some time. It was during the church service that He had answered my question. God had been talking to me all along. When I could not hear His voice He used two of my trusted friends to tell me what I needed to hear. I had to learn to praise Him while *IN* the wilderness rather than focusing on the wilderness itself. It was then that God's blessings in my life came to mind. At that moment I did not have to take hold of God's hand because He took my hand first and led me out of my "wilderness experience".

It is not God's intention for us to find our own way out. To praise Him and thank Him even when we are lost could very well put an end to your "wilderness experience". And it is at the end of this experience that you will encounter God...waiting for you with open arms!

If our words have value that determine our character
then maybe it's time we look at our "checkbook balance".

DAY THIRTY-EIGHT

WORDS

I remember being in elementary school and seeing a poster in our school lunchroom that read: "You are what you eat". Whether that's true or not remains to be seen. Considering my diet at times, I hope the statement is NOT true.

I think a more accurate statement would be: "You are what you *SAY*" because words have so much power and influence. Your words give insight to who you are, therefore the core of a man is revealed through his tongue. We all know that words can build you up and they can tear you down.

Actions can speak louder than words but words themselves can determine our actions. A person with low self-esteem may be the result of harsh words that shattered their sense of worth. But words of encouragement and commendation can strengthen even the weakest foundation of the soul. A mere handful of words can construct or constrict. It is our words that have the power to build or to break.

Consider the effect of words on our lives as similar to balancing a checkbook. Words that are constructive are like deposits into your account. They are profitable and can add value to your net worth. Wounding words are like huge withdrawals that can deplete and diminish your account balance. Your checkbook will have a negative balance if your withdrawals are more than your deposits resulting in insufficient funds. It is the same with spoken words. We take for granted that words are harmless or that words do not wound but verbal statements can either increase or decrease your sense of self-worth.

Words have value that determine our character and reveal who we really are. What is in our hearts will be evidenced by the words we speak. Spoken words of truth and kindness are deposits into a person's heart that are even more valuable than words can ever say.

...the best way to make God laugh is to tell Him what your plans are.

DAY THIRTY-NINE

MAKING GOD LAUGH

Someone once told me that the best way to make God laugh is to tell Him what your plans are. Upon thinking about this statement I realized that I have made God laugh many times in my life. One reason is because by nature I am a planner. I like to at least have an idea of where I am in my life and where I'm going. There have been times when I have had to laugh at myself based on some of the plans I made versus the plans God had in mind for my life. Here is an example of one of my "big plans" that no one knows about except me and God: I once (very) briefly contemplated becoming a Flight Attendant for a major airline thinking of how cool it would be to fly around the world, meet interesting people, all while earning an income. The moment I heard that flight attendants must know how to swim, my "big plans" were shattered especially since I can't even float in any body of water! I can only imagine God bent over in laughter at that bright idea.

If you really sit and think about it, many of us have had times when our lives have gone in a totally different direction than what we would have thought or planned for ourselves.

I believe that God doesn't mind us making plans for our lives, but I also believe that He wants us to remain flexible to the plans <u>He</u> has for us. Even though becoming a flight attendant was not God's plan for me, if that was His plan, He would NEVER set me up to fail! Allow me to encourage you, God knows the plans He has for you. Trusting Him is your only job.

Am I still a planner? Yes, I am. But I try to remind myself that no matter what direction I may try to steer my life, I still must let God do the driving. He does not have to follow my map; it is me who must follow His. No matter what my plans are, no matter how many "bright ideas" I get, and no matter what roads I choose to travel, it is only the plans of God that will ultimately lead me in the way that I should go.

If God really does laugh when I tell Him what my plans are, then I thank God that He has a sense of humor, because as a planner I seem to make God laugh all the time...

We can make our plans, but the Lord determines our steps. (Proverbs 16:9)

Oftentimes we don't see God because we don't look for Him.
His love for us is revealed every single day.

DAY FORTY

EXPERIENCING GOD'S LOVE IN EVERYDAY LIFE

When was the last time you heard birds chirping early in the morning? When was the last time you noticed a trail of ants scurrying on a sidewalk in search for food? When was the last time you felt a gentle breeze while walking to your car after a long day at work? These are questions that I simply cannot answer. Why not? It is because I have not taken the time to do so.

So often it is the little things that go unnoticed. But just because things are not seen does not mean that they do not exist. I remember when I used to be able to smell rain when a storm was approaching. Now when I see dark clouds in the horizon, the smell of rain is the last thing I think about. It is not that it no longer exists, it is simply that it goes unnoticed.

We can experience God in so many ways if we would just take the time to see Him, hear Him, or feel Him. As a child I used to think God was sitting up high too busy to be concerned about what concerned me. I used to think that some things I had to figure out on my own because God was too busy with bigger things than what was going on with me. It was not until I got to really know Him that I realized that some of the tiniest things in my everyday life represented His presence.

One summer day I decided to look for God. I had no plan in mind of what to look for nor did I have a strategy of how to find Him. I decided to go for an afternoon run in my neighborhood, eat a small meal afterwards, and then start my quest to find my Creator. Usually when I go for a run, my mind is focused on how far I want to run and how long it might take to finish. But on this particular day my run was different.

This day was particularly warm as the sun was beaming high in the sky. My usual routine is to run to the halfway mark and immediately head back home with no break in between. But for some reason, I stopped halfway. I heard birds chirping in the trees for the first time in a long time. Instinctively I looked up and saw leaves in the trees blowing in the wind. I could even hear and feel a gentle breeze on a warm summer day. I then looked down and saw tiny ants moving rapidly on the sidewalk.

The combination of birds chirping and leaves blowing in a light wind made me realize that I was hearing God, seeing God, and feeling God right where I stood. I came to understand that even though I had not taken the time to see God in the simplest of things, God was still there. He was there even when I failed to notice Him. Not until I took the time to stop and see God in my everyday life that I could appreciate how awesome He truly is.

God presented Himself to me in the pure innocence of tiny ants running around on a sidewalk. He spoke to me through the sound of a light wind with a glowing sun on hot a summer day. He allowed me to feel His presence through a gentle breeze that swept across my face. When I looked for God, I found Him in so many astonishing ways that I knew He had been with me all along.

Many times we look for God in grand gestures and significant signs but God's love is evident in the smallest things and the simplest scenarios. Oftentimes we don't see God because we don't look for Him. His love for us is revealed every single day. If we look for God, we will find Him. If we listen for His voice, we can hear it. We have the ability to experience God's love in our everyday lives…if we would just take the time to notice.

Conclusion

It is my hope that the love of Christ was ever present during this journey. May you continue to feel His love in your everyday life. I wish you God's absolute best...From the heart!

About The Author

Sharon's resolve is to bless as many people as possible by relating simple scenarios to spiritual and Christian concepts. It is with joy that she shares God's light and God's love. It is her mission to impart the heart of God with her words — from her heart to yours.

Loyalty to family and friends mean the most to Sharon. She is a loving daughter to her parents, Hilbert Sr. and Mary Guillory, her brothers, Hilbert Jr., Hilton, and twin sister, Karon. She truly misses her deceased brother, Kevin. She enjoys spending time with her nieces and nephews, Aaron, Ashley, Briana, Kevin, Sister-in-Law, Julie and great niece, Aubree.

Share your heart with me:

www.heart2yours.com

CPSIA information can be obtained
at www.ICGtesting.com
Printed in the USA
FFOW04n0605190417